Original title:
Treetop Thoughts

Copyright © 2025 Creative Arts Management OÜ
All rights reserved.

Author: Wyatt Kensington
ISBN HARDBACK: 978-1-80567-383-5
ISBN PAPERBACK: 978-1-80567-682-9

Sanctuary of the Skybound

In the branches, we conspire,
Squirrels plotting in attire.
They wear their acorn hats with flair,
While birds give gossip from mid-air.

Secret meetings, leaves our screen,
Raccoons argue, who is seen?
A contest of the silliest puns,
While the owls hoot, counting runs.

A butterfly claims it's a king,
But can't remember anything.
The bees buzz with a wicked jest,
'We make honey, they're never blessed!'

An acorn falls, we all just duck,
Nature's way of saying 'What luck!'
With laughter echoing far and wide,
In this high retreat, we take our pride.

The Poetry of Perching

I saw a squirrel dance, oh what a sight,
With acorns in paws, he took off in flight.
A bird gave a squawk, quite like a cat,
And joined in the fun, wearing her hat.

A branch decided to wiggle and sway,
While ants held a meeting on what to say.
The wind whispered jokes, just out of reach,
As leaves started laughing, their own little speech.

Unraveled in Leafy Embrace

A raccoon plays tag with a sneaky racquet,
While owls in the trees hoot sweet little packets.
The sun peeked through, like a shy little kid,
And giggled with branches that twisted and slid.

A parrot told tales that made everyone roar,
While bees made the rounds with a dance on the floor.
Together they twirled, in a leafy parade,
In a funny little world, where all thoughts were made.

The Stillness of the Heights

In the quiet above, I heard a bird's joke,
He rustled some leaves and then deftly spoke.
The stillness was thick; then a grunt broke the peace,
A raccoon bumbling, looking for fleece.

A high-flying feather fluffed up in the breeze,
Tickling the grasses and bending the trees.
While up above clouds were marshmallows proud,
Making soft puffs that gathered a crowd.

From the Canopy's Embrace

Oh, the laughter of leaves as they gossip and cheer,
A chipmunk's delight as he shares a cold beer.
The sun blinks jauntily through branches so wide,
While branches whisper secrets with mischief and pride.

Sprinkling down sounds from the rustle of fun,
The canopy dances, their work is not done.
With critters rehearsing their next big charade,
Underneath the tall trees, a magic parade.

Sunlit Soliloquies

In the branches, squirrels prance,
Doing their odd little dance.
Chasing shadows, they create,
A fun show for the feathered state.

A parrot squawks a silly tune,
While raccoons plot beneath the moon.
A woodpecker's tapping beats,
Keeps rhythm with the dancing feats.

A monkey swings with comic flair,
Lobbing nuts without a care.
The sun smiles down on this display,
As laughter colors all the day.

The Language of Leaves

Leaves whisper secrets on the breeze,
Discussing gossip with the trees.
One says, 'Look at that odd chap,'
A squirrel wearing a leafy cap.

The wind joins in with a cheeky laugh,
As branches bend, they're quite the staff.
They giggle at a wandering snail,
That's lost its way on the leafy trail.

Acorns chuckle, rolling free,
Playing games of hide and seek.
While seedlings stretch and play their part,
In this leafy, lively art.

Timberline Whispers

Up high, where the pine trees sway,
A bluebird jokes about the day.
With tiny twirls and merry hops,
He flits and flutters, never stops.

The cedar grumbles in a yawn,
'Why do the branches always fawn?'
While moles below in cozy holes,
Trade funny tales with earthy trolls.

A crow caws loud, 'Wings are great,
But can't you fly without that weight?'
And all around, the laughter rings,
In this realm where nature sings.

Flights of Fancy

A duck in shades takes to the sky,
With feathery friends who laugh on by.
The air is filled with giggly squawks,
As turkeys strut in fancy talks.

A bumblebee buzzes with delight,
As flowers join in the banter bright.
'Why do you buzz?' a flower asks,
'Can't you see we're wearing masks?'

Each flower dons its quirkiest hue,
In this party, what fun to pursue!
As butterflies flutter in gleeful flight,
In a world that's whimsical and bright.

Soliloquies of the Swaying Trees

In the breeze, they dance so free,
Leaves gossiping about you and me.
A nut fell down, oh what a test,
Squirrels giggle, 'We are the best!'

Branches wave with playful flair,
'Who's that below? Do they even care?'
A bird squawks, 'You're blocking my sun!'
The trees reply, 'Well, this is fun!'

Songs of the Skyward

Climbing high with a leafy sigh,
Wind whistling tunes as they fly by.
A crow caws, 'What's the plan today?'
The oaks reply, 'Let's play and sway!'

A leaf fashion show, oh what a sight,
Colors and shapes, a pure delight!
Sapling giggles at their tall kin,
'Watch my twirl!' then falls with a spin.

In the Embrace of Greenery

A twig just cracked, was it a joke?
All bark and no bite, said the oak.
The pines chuckled, 'We're evergreen!'
Their needles prick with a playful sheen.

'Come sit a while,' whispers a vine,
'Just don't mind the spider, he's fine!'
A ladybug floats in, looks around,
'Do you think I'm the cutest on ground?'

Whispers Among the Leaves

A squirrel scampers with a grand plan,
To steal a nut right from a bran.
"Hey, watch out!" the branches say,
But he just giggles and runs away.

Sunlight dances on the forest floor,
The trees are laughing, 'Let's hear more!'
A gust comes through, all shake and shimmy,
'Oh dear, it's getting quite whippy and whimsy!'

Nature's Quiet Conversations

Leaves whisper secrets, soft and light,
Squirrels roll dice in the glow of twilight.
Birds wear ties, debating their fate,
While a snail holds court, never in a hurry, not irate.

Dancing shadows play hide and seek,
A raccoon in a hat thinks he's so unique.
The winds giggle, tickling the trees,
As branches sway, played by a gentle breeze.

Echoes of the Emerald Heights

Bumblebees march, all in a line,
Arguing over the best type of thyme.
A peacock struts, wearing vibrant flair,
While frogs pull pranks from their lily pad lair.

Owls give wild looks, wearing spectacles,
With wisdom wrapped in a cloak of jest, perhaps,
The chirps of crickets, a nightly cheer,
As fireflies dance, bringing laughter near.

Poised on the Limbs of Day

A cat perched high, plotting a leap,
Daring a dog to disturb her sleep.
Clouds drift by with a fluffy grin,
Chasing the sun, a playful win-win!

Squirrels throw acorns; it's all a game,
While bunnies giggle without any shame.
Branches sway, trying to juggle their load,
As nature's circus travels down the road.

Lush Reveries

A worm recites poetry in the mud,
While ducks throw parties, what a flood!
Caterpillars plan a parade, oh so grand,
Decked in leaves, they march, just as planned.

The moon peeks in, stifling a yawn,
While raccoons toast to the time of dawn.
With chittering laughter, the night takes flight,
As stars join in, shining oh so bright.

Skyward Whispers

Up high where the squirrels play,
I swear they plot to steal my day.
With acorns stacked in a neat little row,
They laugh and dance, what a show!

Birds gossip in fluttering tones,
Comparing nests made of sticks and stones.
They caw and chirp with such delight,
While I just wish they'd take a flight.

Leaves sway like they own the breeze,
Contemplating life as they tease.
Each rustle a giggle, each flap a jest,
Nature's own comedy, truly the best!

I watch from below and bring out my snack,
But the chipmunks march like a curious pack.
Laughter echoes up to the sun,
In this treetop circus, we've only begun!

Embracing the Skyline

From my perch on this branch, I see,
A world of wonders, oh what glee!
The mailman trips on a little dog,
As I chuckle aloud like a friendly frog.

Clouds drift by, like cotton candy,
Making my thoughts feel light and dandy.
The city below is a bustling fair,
Where people hurry, unaware of air!

The pigeons strut, like they own the scene,
Making the sidewalks their little cuisine.
They coo and compete for the best crumb,
As I laugh from above, feeling quite numb.

Oh, how I love this lofty view,
With endless antics from me to you.
Life's a riot in the sky so bright,
Where each day is filled with pure delight!

The Art of Looking Up

I practiced my gaze, a skill so rare,
Staring up like I haven't a care.
Gnarly branches stretch like silly arms,
Their twists and turns hold the best charms.

The sun peeks through with a cheeky wink,
As I ponder just how much they think.
Do they envy the clouds drifting by?
Or wish for wings, oh me, oh my!

A squirrel zooms past in a furry flash,
Chasing the wind, making a splash.
He pauses to nibble on something gross,
And I can't help but shout, "You're a brave little host!"

I marvel at nature and all her schemes,
In this canvas above, I'm lost in dreams.
Each moment drips with humor's delight,
In this whimsical world, I take flight!

Leafy Epiphanies

Leaves chat in colors, so bright and bold,
Sharing funny tales of the wind they hold.
One whispers softly about its last flight,
When it swirled like a dancer in midday light.

The sun tickles each blade with rays,
While critters bustle in a frenzied haze.
Ants march in line, a hilarious troop,
In their tiny world, they're the big scoop!

Up here, I catch all the playful glances,
Nature's own game of spontaneous dances.
Each rustle is laughter, each gust a cheer,
In this leafy realm, there's nothing to fear.

So join the chorus of giggles and glee,
As the branches sway, wild and free.
In the trees, life's a wacky parade,
Where every moment is one joyously made!

Skyward Reveries

Squirrels plotting mischief loud,
Nuts for a feast, they gather proud.
Birds tweet gossip, quite the chatter,
Who's stealing seeds? Oh, what a matter!

Sunlight dances on the green,
A leaf drops down, but where's the queen?
A raccoon's voice, a surprise guest,
In tree debates, he claims he's best!

Wind swings like a playful child,
Branches sway, oh how they've smiled.
"Who moved my acorn?" shouts a gopher,
Nature's antics, never a loafler.

High above, a nest pan's view,
Three baby birds, a chaos crew.
With a chirp, they claim the sky,
Their lunchtime dance, oh, watch 'em fly!

Canopy Dreams

Up in the air, where silliness reigns,
Laughter echoes down the lanes.
A squirrel wears a tiny hat,
While mocking the owl with a silly spat.

Fruits hang low, they sway and roll,
The raccoon seeks, on a fruit stroll.
Chasing shadows, making a scene,
In this green circus, they're all quite keen.

Chipmunks race in twirling prance,
As beetles join the wiggly dance.
"Watch my flips!" a little frog yells,
In this great height, joy truly swells.

Clouds drifting by, a pun-filled sky,
Who makes the best joke? Give it a try!
A feathered crowd sits with delight,
Imagining flying in a humor flight!

Echoes in the Branches

In branches soft, where whispers cling,
The breeze carries tales of spring.
"Yo! Who took my last acorn?" cries,
The far-off laughter from the skies.

A fox trots in, with a prancing gait,
Betting on who'll win the great plate.
A butterfly challenges the breeze,
"Let's race high up, oh, if you please!"

Underneath, ants weave tight lines,
Making paths to their lunch designs.
A grasshopper jokes, "What's in a name?"
"I'd win a contest in 'Jumping Fame!'"

Wind chimes rustle, a song so sweet,
While nature dances, light on its feet.
Echoes of mirth adorn the glade,
Underneath, a symphony's made!

The View from Above

From high up here, oh what a sight,
Mice slip by, what a funny fright.
"Did you see that?" chirps a wren,
As she tells the tale again and again.

Clouds drift past, soft and bold,
The sun plays peekaboo, bright and gold.
An eagle swoops, what a surprise,
With a wink, he gives trees the eyes!

Raccoons giggle under the stars,
Planning their party, but no guitars.
A leaf falls down, land on a gnome,
"Looks like forest gath'ring at my home!"

High above, where the world twirls round,
Laughter reigns without a sound.
Every branch holds secrets dear,
As nature smiles and fills with cheer!

Wisdom Flowing with the Wind

Squirrels plot with acorn might,
They trick the birds in broad daylight.
Branches sway with laughter loud,
Leaves chuckle 'neath the cloud.

Owls nap while others chat,
Raccoons debate, which tree is fat.
The breeze carries gossip far,
Like gossip at the local bar.

Branches creak with ancient wit,
As chipmunks dance, they never quit.
The canopy's a vast delight,
Full of wisdom, oh what a sight!

Breezes whisper to the leaves,
Come join us, everyone believes.
With every gust, a new tale spins,
Nature's comedy, where fun begins.

A Watcher's Rapture

Perched above, I sip the sky,
Birds zoom past, oh my, oh my!
Watching ants with narrow fates,
This vantage point, it captivates.

A butterfly flutters with flair,
As I chuckle, without a care.
What's the dog thinking, down there?
Should I yell, or be aware?

The sun dips low, a blazing ball,
Trees giggle, lest they fall.
In this leafy, lofty throne,
Observing life, I'm never alone.

My throne of branches sways and creaks,
Every peek brings laughter peaks.
Nature's antics from afar,
Who knew trees could be the star?

Dreams Between the Branches

Crickets sing their nighttime song,
While owls hoot, all night long.
Mist mingles with the starry gleam,
Where dreams float like a silly dream.

A raccoon dreams of shiny things,
While ghostly shadows start to swing.
Squirrels whisper secrets low,
As moonlight filters through the glow.

Twinkling stars in leafy beds,
Where rivers weave through sleepy heads.
Naps are taken, laughter spry,
In leafy chambers, dreams can fly.

When dawn breaks, the giggles cease,
And sleepy limbs find their peace.
But come nightfall, ah what glee,
In the treetops' jubilee!

Silhouettes Against the Sky

Branches twist in shadow play,
As sunshine bids the trees to sway.
Kites drift high, laughter fills the air,
While all around, the little critters share.

Bees brigade with funny bounces,
While flowers sway in silly flounces.
From my perch, I can't help but grin,
Life below, what a wild din!

The sunset spills its orange cheer,
As chirps and chats embark from near.
Each rustle tells a tale of fun,
A tapestry before the night begun.

As darkness blankets, joy won't fade,
For every tree a role has played.
Silhouettes dance through starlit nooks,
Here's to life in nature's books!

The Breeze's Gentle Embrace

Up high where the squirrels dare to prance,
The wind whispers secrets that make branches dance.
A leaf tickles a bird, makes it squawk with surprise,
The bugs hold a meeting while dodging fast flies.

Sunlight giggles as it filters down bright,
While shadows play tag, trying to take flight.
The whispers of leaves tell jokes oh so sly,
As acorns drop down, like a small sky-high pie.

High Above the World

In a world of tall tales and branches so wide,
A crow wears a hat made of twigs with great pride.
He struts on the high wire, a laugh in his call,
Claiming that up here, he is best of them all.

A raccoon in PJs thinks he's quite the sight,
Hanging upside down, feeling quite light.
The sun throws a spotlight on antics so wild,
As owls roll their eyes at the antics of the child.

Branches of Contemplation

The branches convene for their laughter-filled chats,
While monkeys swing by wearing their snazzy hats.
A twig with some sass claims it's the best seat,
As wisdom flows down to the roots and the beet.

An old owl presides, hooting puns with delight,
As sunlight flickers, making shadows take flight.
The wind pulls a branch, gives it a gentle shove,
This meeting at height spreads good vibes and love.

Reflections from the Canopy

From up here, the world looks both silly and grand,
As leaves share stories no one can quite understand.
A branch bows politely, offering shade,
While a twig asks a flower how much it has paid.

Jokes fly like birds, from the height of the green,
While pine cones roll down, causing quite the scene.
From the top of the tree, life's amusing and bright,
Where laughter is plenty, and worries take flight.

A Symphony of Foliage

In leafy halls where laughter grows,
A squirrel's dance, a nutty show.
He juggles acorns, a clumsy feat,
While birds nearby mock his shaky retreat.

Up high, the branches sway and creak,
A raccoon shimmies, feeling sleek.
He trips on twigs, then tumbles down,
The forest roars with a giggly sound.

Chirping tunes, the owls dismay,
They hoot at mischief, come what may.
A chorus tops the windy peaks,
Where nature's jesters play hide-and-seek.

With every gust, a prank takes flight,
Grasshoppers dance in sheer delight.
Each branch's chatter, a witty quip,
In this green world, we all let slip.

Above the Grounded Home

Perched upon the leafy stage,
A crow recites his ancient sage.
He caws out puns with grand finesse,
While ants below just shake and stress.

Swaying in the sun-kissed air,
A parrot's jokes cause quite a scare.
He echoes laughter, shrill and bright,
As the squirrels launch a nutty flight.

Up high they play, that feathered gang,
With acorns bouncing as they sang.
The branches laugh, a rustling cheer,
As critters join, their spirit clear.

With each soft breeze, tales unfold,
Of daring deeds and laughs retold.
A life aloft, a jolly spree,
Where fun and folly roam so free.

Beyond the Nesting Place

In the canopies, where whispers flow,
A wise old owl puts on a show.
He tells of mice that wore "high hats,"
And turtles racing jittery bats.

A breeze brings giggles from the leaves,
As beetles practice acrobatic thieves.
They tumble down, to scatter seeds,
In laughter's wake, the forest feeds.

Up on high, where daylight plays,
The sunbeams tickle, make us daze.
A wispy flight of dragonflies,
Hold court above the velvet skies.

With every rustle, each tiny squeak,
Stories emerge, both bold and cheek.
In nature's court, whimsical hearts,
Find joy in fun, as laughter starts.

Nature's Lofty Thoughts

Above the world, where giggles soar,
A chipmunk shares his snack galore.
He munches while telling cheeky tales,
Of tree-climbing cats that leave funny trails.

High in the branches, a crow makes plans,
To steal a snack from picnic fans.
With a flap and a caw, he dives and zips,
But lands on the ground, collecting quips.

Each rustle there, a friendly jest,
A world where every critter's blessed.
The leaves can't help but shake and grin,
As laughter bubbles, where vines begin.

In leafy realms, mischief flows,
With acorns and twigs, their humor grows.
All together, above we find,
A jolly dance of the woodland kind.

Aerial Confessions

Up here in the branches, life's a game,
Birds gossip and squirrels are never the same.
Leaves flutter gossip, the gossip's all true,
And acorns have secrets, who knew they could chew?

A branch thought it's clever, but broke with a crack,
A dance with the wind, it got quite the smack.
The sky laughs loudly, it's full of delight,
As we swing in the breezes, just out of plain sight.

Dance of the Swaying Boughs

Boughs bend and sway in a merry old dance,
While critters below just miss their big chance.
A raccoon tries to waltz, but ends in a tumble,
While we're up here giggling, oh, how they fumble!

The sun gives a wink to the leaves on the way,
As shadows below shout, 'We want to play!'
Branches fall into rhythm, a sway and a twist,
While nature's lost dancers just can't quite exist.

High Above the Ground

In the canopy chatter, it's never too tame,
With crickets as speakers, the jokes all aim.
A leaf whispered softly, it's ticklish for sure,
While the squirrel just chuckled, found humor pure!

High in the boughs, we put on a show,
With squirrels as acrobats, stealing the glow.
The world looks so silly, from up in the trees,
Where gravity's stubborn, but laughter's a breeze.

Perspectives from the Perch

From our leafy seat, we view the world wide,
While ants march below with their little pride.
The flowers are laughing, the grass shakes and quakes,
As we throw down a twig, for a giggle, it wakes.

Oh, the cats down below, think they're king of the street,
While we're tossing acorns—who said they were sweet?
From up here, we plan pranks on our ground-level friends,

With a wink and a giggle, the laughter just blends.

Horizons of Thought

High above the bustling crowd,
A squirrel's speech, slightly loud.
He shouts of acorns, tales untold,
Knows how the winds can break the cold.

A bird joins in, with feathers bright,
Critiques the clouds, a comical sight.
With every flap, a punchline flies,
Both laugh at humans under skies.

Branches sway, a leafy stage,
Nature's comedians, share their page.
Jokes of nuts and rainy days,
In this lofty realm, laughter plays.

So when you gaze to heights so sweet,
Remember the fun where treetops meet.

The Calm in the Upper Air

In the canopy, a dance of glee,
Leaves rustle, a whispering spree.
A raccoon winks, with mischief pure,
Life's antics, the best allure.

A breeze tickles branches with flair,
While pigs on swings forget their dare.
The calm, it seems, is a playful tease,
As squirrels juggle, aiming to please.

Each rustling sound, a joyful jest,
In this high place, they never rest.
Life's simple joys, the punchlines ring,
Nature's laughter, an endless spring.

Check your worries, leave them below,
In the high air, just let them go.

Silent Conversations with the Sky

Up here, the clouds share a wink,
Dreamy thoughts flow with no ink.
A sparrow narrates tales of delight,
While sunbeams play, tickling light.

Whispers of winds, giggling loud,
Jokes traded high, above the crowd.
Each gust of air, a playful jest,
In silent chats, they are the best.

A chattering chipmunk spills the tea,
On how the earth's done with the spree.
The sky just nods, with glimmers bright,
As laughter echoes into the night.

These moments are gold, light as air,
In the quiet, we find the rare.

Unseen Pathways

Wandering paths of leafy dreams,
Where sunlight dances, giggles and beams.
A hedgehog snores on a warm stone,
Dreaming of jellybeans, all alone.

Above, a crow croaks a witty line,
Twisting tales of her secret vine.
With each flap, she makes it clear,
That life is better up here, my dear.

While rustling leaves play hide and seek,
Every snap sounds like a cheeky peek.
In the forest's grip, laughter's key,
On unseen pathways, we are free.

So climb up high, lose the frown,
Join the jesters, never drown.

the Freedom of High Vistas

Up in the air, without a care,
Squirrels plot, and birds declare,
Every gust, a breezy ride,
Waving branches, nature's slide.

A raccoon in glasses, reading a map,
Ponders the route for a long afternoon nap.
While down below, the ants march along,
What a wild world, where odd things belong!

Pine cones tumble, a comical fall,
A dance of leaves, an aerial ball.
And the clouds above, a fluffy parade,
In this lofty realm, no plans laid.

So let's laugh with the chant of the breeze,
As nature conspires with quirky unease.
For in the heights, we find our cheer,
Where the silliest thoughts seem brilliantly clear.

Hidden Thoughts in Leafy Labyrinths

In the shade where whispers twine,
Leaves conceal a secret line.
Rabbits giggle, shared their lore,
About the fox who tripped before.

Shadows dance on the forest floor,
Wishing for snacks, what's in store?
Mice sprinkle breadcrumbs for a feast,
While sneaky raccoons munch the least.

A butterfly mocks, flits with delight,
"To dance with flowers? Quite a sight!"
They swap their hats, a leaf for a crown,
Nature's jesters, never a frown.

So in this maze, where laughter leads,
Joy grows wild, and chaos feeds.
In hidden thoughts, the fun explodes,
Among leafy paths, the humor erodes.

Suspension of Solitude

Up on a branch, a goldfinch sings,
Twirling around, on invisible strings.
A snail sips tea on a mushroom cap,
"Mind the drip!" he exclaims with a flap.

A lone sloth swings, at a leisurely pace,
Takes a moment to check his own face.
The wise old owl gives a wink and a nod,
"Hang on there, buddy, this is quite odd."

Cotton candy clouds, a sweet little dream,
Squirrels flipping pancakes, a breakfast theme.
With a flip and a flop, they aim for the sky,
While below, ants decide to give pie a try.

In solitude, where giggles reign,
Each little creature joins the same lane.
As laughter echoes from leaf to breeze,
Together they swing, with giggles that please.

The Quietude Above

High on a perch, where giggles reign,
A clamoring of critters goes insane.
The chipmunks argue about who's the best,
While the tree frogs practice their stand-up jest.

A bear with a hat tries to find his style,
Wobbling on branches, full of guile.
The wild boar rolls down, such an elegant fall,
He grumbles and grunts, "I've seen better ball!"

Atop the world, strange tales unfurl,
On twigs and leaves, the laughter whirls.
A parade of oddities, smiling away,
In quietude above, where fun leads the play.

So lift your spirits, let worries cease,
In this lofty realm, we find our peace.
With every breezy chuckle and jest,
This sweet sanctuary is simply the best.

Brushing the Clouds

Up high where the giggles float,
Squirrels dance in their bright fur coats.
They trade jokes with the wayward breeze,
While birds share puns with rustling leaves.

A wise owl chuckles, donning a hat,
"Who brings snacks? This cloud is flat!"
The sun slips by with a playful wink,
As raindrops drop and make us think.

Clouds wear mustaches, a fluffy sight,
Fog rolls in, giving us a fright.
Dancing shadows, a whimsical show,
Where laughter bounces and breezes blow.

In this lighthearted, floating realm,
We're all captains at the clouds' helm.
As nature plays its silly tune,
Join the merry laughter 'neath the moon.

The Wisdom of Skyward Paths

The ladder to the sky is tall,
With whispers of wisdom that brightly call.
A squirrel leads with a quirky grin,
As thoughts tumble like acorns in the wind.

"Step lightly here, the clouds might giggle,
And they'll tease your shoes till you wiggle."
Tree trunks nod, sharing secrets of old,
In this high place where stories unfold.

Each branch is a stage for playful fun,
Where raccoons juggle and squirrels run.
They gather to share a good old tale,
As clouds drift by in a fluffy sail.

The skyward paths invite us to play,
With laughter echoing all the way.
Join the summit of whimsical highs,
And let your worries float to the skies.

Breezy Reflections

In the breeze, a mirror wide,
Shows reflections of joy we cannot hide.
Leaves gossip about the ground below,
While the sun giggles in a golden glow.

"Muffins or pollen?" a bumblebee hums,
"Let's start a bakery—not just for crumbs!"
As gusty winds swirl with cheerful notes,
Nature's orchestra plays, and each one floats.

Clouds wear smiles, floating up there,
Combining raindrops with silly flair.
The moon rolls in, giving a wink,
Turning the serious into the pink.

Let's dance on the soft green grass,
As the trees sway and join the class.
Life's reflections are full of cheer,
In this breezy space, we've nothing to fear.

Songs of the Avian Choir

The birds gather for a concert today,
With each chirp turning mundane to play.
A canary hums a catchy tune,
As a parrot dances beneath the moon.

"Hey there, buddy! Can you keep time?"
A crow calls out, sharp as a rhyme.
The sparrows twist in a comedy swirl,
While the robins twirl and give it a whirl.

Feathers fluff in a grand parade,
As owls roll their eyes, a little dismayed.
"Do they ever stop?" they hoot with glee,
In this avian band, everyone's free.

The sky's the limit when voices unite,
With giggles that soar, taking flight.
So join the choir, raise your voice high,
With laughter and joy, let's sing and fly!

Owls and Observations

In the night, wise owls stare,
Judging squirrels with flair.
They hoot and they cackle,
As raccoons start to wrangle.

The trees become their stage,
As they turn another page.
With a wink and a nod,
They laugh at the odd.

A little branch wobbles here,
Causing a feathered cheer.
With each twist and turn,
The giggles they earn.

So up they go, quite spry,
While other critters just sigh.
For in the treetop show,
There's laughter below.

Climbing Inner Peaks

Little squirrels in a race,
Trying hard to find their place.
They leap from branch to branch,
In a wild, comical dance.

With nuts clutched in their paws,
They're masters of faux pas.
One trips on a twig,
And gives that tree a jig!

High above the forest floor,
They scheme and plot for more.
"Just climb a little higher,"
One shouts, starting a fire.

Then down comes a plump blue jay,
Bringing along the sunny day.
With twitters and chirps, they thrive,
Treetop acrobatics come alive!

A Harmony Among the Heights

Above the world, in leafy shrouds,
A band of critters sing aloud.
A raccoon with a tambourine,
While a wren plays on, so keen.

The harmony is sweet and bright,
As hazel eyes glow in the night.
With mischief in their hearts, they play,
Creating tunes to rule the day.

A little owl joins on cue,
With a solo, "Hoo hoo!"
The shadows sway in time and beat,
As nature's jesters dance on feet.

With laughter echoing through the trees,
The air is filled with joyful breeze.
In this kooky high parade,
The fun never seems to fade!

Soft Shadows, Bright Minds

In the shade where sunlight drips,
Clever thoughts hop like little quips.
A turtle joins with a slow grin,
As he watches the chaos begin.

Chirps and chortles fill the air,
While shadows frolic without care.
A chipmunk with a hat so grand,
Directs the show with a tiny hand.

As laughter bounces off the leaves,
Even the oldest tree believes.
Wisdom finds its place in fun,
As bright minds race under the sun.

So let the laughter soar and glide,
In this leafy, joyful ride.
From soft shadows, tales unwind,
In the funniest of minds.

Entwined in Airy Matters

Swaying branches dance and play,
As squirrels plot a nut buffet.
I swear the leaves all giggle bright,
While chatting with the birds in flight.

A woodpecker knocks, a rhythmic cheer,
Pondering if the sky's too near.
The sun spills laughter, golden gleams,
While clouds float by like silly dreams.

Mischief brews in every breeze,
As insects ride like tiny whizzes.
A butterfly drafts high above,
Seems like a joke, that's full of love.

In a leafy sea, we're all afloat,
Conversations rise like a funny quote.
So here's to thoughts that soar and sing,
In a forest realm where giggles spring.

Where Earth Meets Air

Up where branches pierce the blue,
The birds tell tales that tickle too.
A cheeky breeze runs through the pines,
Whispering secrets, playful signs.

Squirrels wear their acorn hats,
Looking for mischief, like clever cats.
The sun, a jester, beams with mirth,
Painting smiles upon the earth.

A kite wanders, free as can be,
Chasing shadows of a bumblebee.
Laughter echoes among the leaves,
As nature spins its yarns and weaves.

Life is a game high up on high,
With winds that tease and clouds that sigh.
So let's join in this frolicsome air,
And share these moments without a care.

High Altitude Revelations

Perched where giggles meet the sky,
All worries seem to wave goodbye.
Branches stretch in a playful pose,
Chasing dreams where humor flows.

A crow tells jokes with flair and style,
As eagles nod and wink a mile.
While pinecones plot a comedic scheme,
Wrapped in laughter, a silly dream.

That chipmunk thinks he rules the wood,
With twiggy crowns, he feels quite good.
A laugh erupts from leafy thickets,
As frolicsome fun in each nook beckons.

The breeze is light, with jokes to share,
Tickling buds with soft, sweet air.
Let's spin our tales and laugh aloud,
In this lofty realm of a merry crowd.

The Breezy Contemplation

In a world where breezes play,
Thoughts take flight, then drift away.
Clouds don silly hats of white,
As daydreams dance in pure delight.

A robin sings, "What's new today?"
While chattering leaves join the display.
High above, a playful jest,
Leaves chuckle, "We're the very best!"

Tree trunks whisper secrets bold,
Sharing giggles, never old.
Branches wave in bright parade,
Making fun in sunlight's shade.

So let's hoist our laughter high,
And share a grin with passerby.
For where the earth and air collide,
There blooms a humor we can't hide.

Above the World's Noise

High up in the trees, I spy,
Squirrels chatting, oh my, oh my!
They plan their acorns like a heist,
While I munch on snacks, with a grin so wide.

Birds wear sunglasses, it's quite the sight,
They gossip and laugh, what a pure delight!
With each passing leaf, they throw their shade,
As I swing on a branch, unafraid.

The wind whips through, a cheeky breeze,
Tickling my toes, making me wheeze.
I'm the king of this leafy court,
While frogs below hold a loud report.

In this vibrant world, I dance and sway,
The world's below but I'm here to play!
Nature's comedy, so absurd yet true,
Above the noise, I find my view.

Secrets in the Foliage

Whispers glide through the dappled light,
Rabbits fear over picking a fight.
Squirrels point and giggle, oh dear,
What secrets lie hidden? I simply must hear.

Branches creak softly, it's a playhouse,
Raccoons debate, who's the loudest spouse?
A tree stump holds gossip; it's quite the chart,
While the butterflies flutter, playing their part.

A ladybug winks, full of sass,
"Who needs a crowded party? We'll have class!"
With leaves as our cover, we laugh and tease,
In this green cabaret, we do as we please.

Beneath all the chatter, a mystery grows,
In foliage thick, hilarity flows.
From muddy paws to chipmunk cheers,
Here in the wild, we toast with our peers.

Celestial Musings

A bright-eyed owl thinks it's quite absurd,
Why humans act like the silliest bird?
They dress in suits, all sharp and neat,
While I hoot jokes with my veggie treat.

Stars blink above like they're in a race,
I wonder if they ever lose face.
Why chase your tail, when up's where it's at?
Among branches and leaves, I shine like a bat.

Clouds come and go with a fluffy dance,
They argue over who gave rain a chance.
In the cool nighttime breeze, I float and spin,
With a flutter of wings, let the mischief begin.

Cosmic giggles echo in the dark,
As fireflies flash, igniting a spark.
In this canopy realm where laughter flows,
The universe chuckles, and no one knows.

Wings of the Wind

With a gust of glee, the breeze flew through,
Playing tag with birds, it giggled anew.
It tickled the tweeter, made her squawk,
If you've got wings, it's the life of the Hawk!

Down below, bunnies ache to outrun,
The swift little zephyrs, oh what fun!
They hop and they zoom, dodging each gust,
While I dangle my feet, lying in trust.

In these high branches, I hold my court,
While the wind whispers secrets, light and short.
It spins around, tickling my chin,
"Come join the fun, let the games begin!"

With each twist and turn, the branches sway,
Chasing the clouds and wishing to play.
Up here in the heights, I smile with glee,
Wings of the wind, you're the best company!

Floating on Gentle Breezes

Up high where the wild things grin,
A squirrel juggles acorns, what a win!
Birds start a band with a chirpy beat,
While I sip nectar, oh, what a treat!

The leaves are gossiping, oh such drama,
A raccoon's on stage, acting like a llama!
Butterflies giggle, flitting about,
While ants work hard, but oh, they pout!

A breeze tickles cheeks, it's a playful tease,
As I dance with shadows, swaying with ease.
Nature's a joke, always with a twist,
In this high-up haven, I can't resist!

So let's float like dandelions in the sun,
In a world of laughter, we're never done.
With each gentle gust, my worries release,
In this realm of mirth, I find my peace!

Sunlit Meditations

Sunbeams tickle through the leaves,
While bees plot missions, buzzing thieves.
Grasshoppers leap, think they can fly,
But land on my head, oh me, oh my!

The sun makes me squint, it's quite a sight,
A raccoon is snoozing, dreaming of fright.
Clouds play hide-and-seek in the blue,
While squirrels sing ballads, just for a few!

Laying on grass, it's more like a thrill,
A caterpillar's here, making a meal.
Each whisper of wind, a chuckle shared,
Nature's my comic, it's wonderfully squared.

So here's to the laughter, bright and bold,
With sunlit joys that never grow old.
Every rustle and giggle keeps me awake,
In this silly moment, there's much at stake!

Mindful in the Wilderness

In a forest of wonders, I start to ponder,
Where squirrels tell tales of mischief and wonder.
I trip on a twig and tumble down low,
Only to find a frog putting on a show!

Mushrooms like umbrellas, so quirky and bright,
A snail's slow dance is quite a delight.
The trees seem to chuckle, they wiggle in glee,
As I join the parade of the busy bumblebee!

Nature's a stage with a cast full of gags,
The rabbits run past with the sassiest rags.
A sunflower winks, the daisies applaud,
In this wilderness play, I'm never ignored!

With every misstep, I find my own groove,
In a world full of quirks, it's easy to move.
Mindful I wander, with laughter my guide,
In this wild woodland, joy cannot hide!

Harmony in the Canopy

Above in the branches, a jam session starts,
With owls in tuxedos and raccoons with hearts.
The wind strums a tune on the leaves so green,
As I tap my foot to the forest's routine!

Chirping and squeaking, the orchestra plays,
While chipmunks pull pranks in hilarious ways.
A parrot on keys, playing melodies nice,
In this leafy lounge, every nod's a surprise!

The sunbeams are spotlights on mossy old stones,
As laughter erupts from the critters and drones.
With each little twirl, the branches all sway,
Who knew trees had rhythm? Let's dance, come what may!

So here in the canopy, the joy feels so wide,
With nature's own symphony, I'm along for the ride.
In this harmony's bliss, you can't help but smile,
As we groove through the leaves, let's stay for a while!

The Serenity Above

In lofty limbs, where squirrels play,
I ponder life, in a silly way.
Why can't I fly, like birds so free?
But here I am, just stuck in a tree.

A crow nearby scoffs at my plight,
As I juggle acorns with all my might.
A branch breaks off, I start to sway,
Guess gravity doesn't care for my display!

The wind gives a chuckle, a gentle tease,
As leaves dance around like clowns in the breeze.
I wave to the clouds, they wink and go,
It's all in good fun, just a show to bestow.

So up here I stay, with a grin so wide,
Feeling like a king with the sky as my guide.
In this airy realm, laughter takes flight,
Finding joy in the height, a whimsical sight.

Whispers of Green Majesty

In the branches above, a chatty parrot,
He tells me tales in a voice quite garrot.
"Why worry, mate? Just climb higher!"
But now there's a wasp, and my patience is dire!

The leaves are giggling, they wiggle and shake,
I try to look cool, but my balance they take.
With each little stumble, I can't help but grin,
As green folks watch on, my dance they begin!

A raccoon strolls by with his snack in tow,
"Sharing is caring!" I call, but he won't show.
He clutches the crumbs like a treasure of gold,
While I'm stuck here thinking, "I'm way too bold!"

Yet laughter does linger in all of this mess,
For in leafy realms, I feel quite blessed.
Nature's a stage, with whimsy and cheer,
Every mishap above just brings me more beer!

Crafted by the Breeze

With a gust of wind, I'm pushed to the right,
A butterfly giggles, then takes off in flight.
I'm dodging the branches, a dance that's unique,
This tree-top ballet, it's quite the mystique!

I spot a wise owl, with spectacles round,
"Do birds ever trip?" is the thought that I found.
He hoots and he chuckles, "Oh sure, but we soar,
Your style is much funnier; keep giving us more!"

The twigs are my partners, as I spin and twirl,
A woodpecker joins in, "Come on, give it a whirl!"
We sway with a rhythm, a comedy show,
Between beaks and my giggles, the good times just flow.

So here I shall balance, without a care near,
In this crazy ballet, with laughter sincere.
Crafted by breezes, with friends all around,
Life's amusing adventures are always unbound.

The Introspection of the Heights

Perched high on a twig, I muse on my fate,
A squirrel scurries past, oh how fast, how great!
"Am I savvier than him?" I ponder this thought,
Until he drops acorns; I just start to rot.

The sun sneaks in, casting shadows galore,
I wave to the clouds, "Hey, don't block my door!"
They slowly drift by, like thoughts on my mind,
"What's next on this journey? More acorns to find?"

A breeze whispers softly, playing tricks on my hair,
I giggle at whispers, embracing fresh air.
Life's little puzzles are fun to perceive,
Especially when perched where no one would believe.

So here in the canopy, full of delight,
I sip on my wisdom, all day and all night.
In the heights of amusement, I find I belong,
Where the laughter is silly, and thoughts feel so strong!

Lullabies of the Tree Tops

Whispers of leaves sing to the breeze,
Squirrels giggle, dancing with ease.
A woodpecker taps a funny beat,
While ants do the cha-cha on tiny feet.

The sun peeks in through the leafy greens,
While chipmunks count their hidden beans.
Each branch a stage for a critter show,
With acorn hats for the audience below.

Altitude and Attitude

Swaying high on a swaying branch,
Ladybugs flirt, hoping to ranch.
Ravens cruise with flair and sass,
While pigeons try to join the class.

Parrots squawk with a touch of grace,
As lizards strike a goofy pose space.
In the sky, they all seem bold,
Sharing secrets that never get old.

The Air Between the Limbs

A breeze jokes with the fluttering leaves,
While a lone fly tricks the spider who weaves.
Each gust carries laughter through the space,
As branches cradle their funny embrace.

The sun shines bright, creating a show,
As critters huddle, forming a row.
They share tales of socks and lost keys,
While swing-dancing with the cheeky breeze.

Winding Paths in the Sky

Clouds drift by with a silly grin,
While kites take flight, inviting a spin.
Rabbits hop from one branch to the next,
In a puzzling game, they're quite perplexed.

Each path winds up to funny new places,
Where squirrels wear hats and throw small embraces.
With laughter echoing through the blue,
The sky becomes a whimsical view.

Echoes of Nature's Serenity

Up in the branches, a squirrel did sing,
Making a fuss over a shiny old ring.
He thought it a treasure, a crown for his head,
Worn by the birds, but lost in bed.

A woodpecker knocked with a rhythmic beat,
Vying for limelight—beating his feet.
A rabbit hopped by with a curious glance,
'Is that a new dance, or just lost in trance?'

Nearby, a frog croaked, 'I'm a star, look at me!'
While ants formed a line for a tall cup of tea.
In nature's grand play, each role feels just right,
Even when critters can't quite take flight.

The sun peeked through, on this misfit parade,
As shadows of leaves danced, unafraid.
With laughter and joy, this riotous team,
Crafted a day that felt like a dream.

Beneath the Open Void

Frogs wear their pants as they leap through the mud,
While squirrels plan lunch in a grand acorn flood.
With laughter in leaves that giggle and sway,
Who knew the woods had such quirky display?

The trees gossip softly, whispering lies,
About owls who hoot with unflattering ties.
A butterfly flutters, then gets all confused,
Chasing its tail, it feels quite abused.

A raccoon in a mask, quite ready for fame,
Dreams of a stage, 'Oh, how they'll all claim!
The nature show crown, I deserve every bit,
With stars like the sunset, I'll surely be hit!'

So under this sky, mischief does sprout,
Among all the creatures, it's laughter we shout.
An orchestra plays, from branches to ground,
In the symphony of fun, we're forever unbound.

Skybound Fables

A posh little crow snatched a crumb from a plate,
Pretending to dine while he picked at his fate.
His pals were all watching, from near and from far,
'Be careful,' they cawed, 'that's a meeting of stars!'

A puffed-up peacock strutted with pride,
Claiming his feathers were hard to abide.
In the sun's golden glow, fierce battles did weave,
As friends tried to form him a new autumn sleeve.

A chipmunk was busy, dodging around,
Trying to gather the best snacks he found.
But with every nut, he'd stumble and trip,
Ending up giggling, on a banana peel slip!

In the jungle of jests, where nonsense is king,
Misfits unite with the joy that they bring.
Their tales twist and turn, with laughter galore,
In the fables of life, fun opens each door.

Breath of the Wind

The breeze whispered secrets, a tickle on cheeks,
While butterflies chatted, discussing their peaks.
With a gust of pure laughter, the leaves took a twirl,
In the dance of the day, they spun with a whirl.

A wise old tortoise flipped over a stone,
Said, 'Let's race,' but he was racing alone.
As dragonflies darted, they laughed at the sight,
Who knew that the slowpoke could get such a fright?

In the corner, a hedgehog was planning a feast,
With berries and bugs, celebrated, at least.
But someone forgot he just can't let them in,
For it's hard to share when you've bristled your skin!

So under the sky, where all creatures convene,
Every leaf in the wind tells a tale that's unseen.
In nature's own style, joy bubbles and blends,
Creating a laughter that never just ends.

Secrets of the Upper Boughs

In the leafy realm where squirrels play,
Secrets abound in a funny display.
A bird tried to sing, but forgot the tune,
Instead, he hummed way too close to noon.

The branches giggle with each tiny breeze,
While ants wear hats, discussing grand fees.
A sloth in a tie gives the best career tips,
While frogs practice dance moves with wild little flips.

The sun sneaks peeks through the greenery's veil,
Where cheeky raccoons spin tales without fail.
Old owls chuckle at their wise old lore,
As sunbeams chase shadows, and laughter can soar.

So if you look up at the branches' embrace,
You might just see joy in this bustling place.
Each leaf holds a giggle, a wink, or a sigh,
In the top of the trees, where the spirits fly high.

Perched in Serenity

Perched on a limb with a sense of delight,
A pigeon plays chess with a sprite in the night.
A parrot's loud laughter fills the air with glee,
While a turtle in sunglasses orders iced tea.

A robin recounts tales from the ground,
While butterflies flitter, spinning 'round and 'round.
A squirrel does yoga, oh what a sight!
His zen in the branches brings pure, silly light.

The sun tickles leaves with a playful caress,
While beavers in bow ties debate who's the best.
A frog on a branch sports a crown made of fluff,
Declaring that sitting is simply enough.

With laughter and banter, the upper boughs sway,
In a world full of whimsy, come join in the play.
For perched in this haven, let giggles be our guide,
In a kingdom of humor, let joy be our pride.

Dancing with the Wind

Up in the air where the breezes frolic,
A crow shows off moves that are simply symbolic.
With a twirl and a spin, he takes to the sky,
As a grasshopper judges, declaring him spry.

Bushes are humming, and laughter's awake,
As crickets compose songs by the old wooden lake.
A branch bends to giggle, whispering tales,
While a chipmunk narrates his bounty of snails.

The wind winks and twirls, with sass and with style,
As a dog in a top hat struts by with a smile.
"Let's dance!" booms a voice from a cloud overhead,
And the leaves join the party, all worries now shed.

So come take a twirl by the twinkling light,
Where shadows are dancing, giving joy to the night.
In the world of the trees and the gusts that do spin,
Every laugh is a waltz, let the fun now begin.

Skylark Musings

A skylark sat high, sipping morning's brew,
With a grin on his beak, all bright and askew.
He pondered the clouds and rehearsed silly jokes,
While nearby, a goat held court with some folks.

The breeze played piano, the leaves were the strings,
As a goat in a cape proclaimed wondrous things.
"Life's a grand circus, and I'm the head clown!
Watch me tightrope walk while I'm wearing a gown!"

A squirrel chimed in with a nutty old rhyme,
Dancing on branches, oh, isn't it prime?
While flowers chuckled at their vivid hue,
As the daisies debated if purple's the new blue.

With each little chuckle, the branches just sway,
Creating a chorus of joy in their play.
So if ever you wander under boughs wide and deep,
Know laughter's the treasure that the treetops keep.

Dreams Nestled in Green

Squirrels gossip in the leaves,
They share tales of acorn thieves.
A bird trips over a twig,
Laughing at its own big dig.

The breeze plays peek-a-boo with flies,
While branches tickle the bluest skies.
A frog leaps high to join the fun,
But lands too close to the bright sun.

The owls declare an evening dance,
With mice who've come to take a chance.
Every leaf has a secret to share,
As laughter echoes through the air.

With every rustle, there's a cheer,
In this green realm, let's leave our fear.
With dreams afloat like dandelion seeds,
Let's spin our tales among the reeds.

Up Where the Wild Things Are

High above in the wooden maze,
The raccoons hold their sneaky gaze.
A party starts when night descends,
With critters all around as friends.

A bear in shades plays the guitar,
And the rabbits dance, they're quite bizarre.
While owls spin tales both wise and wide,
The moonlight shines as their guide.

The skunks provide their fragrant show,
While fireflies play tag in the glow.
And every tree, a stage afire,
Where nature's humor never tires.

So join the fun, don't miss the ride,
In this great wild, we take great pride.
With laughter echoing through the air,
Let's shake our tails without a care!

Light and Shadows in the Throne of Branches

Up above, a giggle floats,
From chubby squirrels in tiny coats.
They play hide and seek in warm sunbeams,
While ants march by with silly dreams.

A wily fox dons a crown of leaves,
Sipping dew from what nature weaves.
The shadows dance as the sun dips low,
While branches sway in a merry flow.

The acorns fall with a perfect plop,
As a sleepy owl begins to hop.
Each twirl of the leaves is a song,
In this forest realm where we belong.

With every chuckle and every cheer,
Nature's court is full of good cheer.
So let's raise a toast to this leafy spree,
In the throne of branches, wild and free!

Gaze of the Wanderer

Atop the limbs, a traveler stands,
With curious eyes and eager hands.
The world below seems small and neat,
As branches dance beneath his feet.

He sees the world from heights so grand,
As sunflower faces wave and stand.
A caterpillar rolls with a sigh,
Dreaming of wings, and wanting to fly.

He giggles at the busy bees,
Who buzz around like tiny keys.
Unlocking secrets among the blooms,
As laughter rings through blossomed rooms.

In this high place, whimsy prevails,
And every breeze tells funny tales.
So come along, join the view,
Where wanderers dream, and skies are blue.

www.ingramcontent.com/pod-product-compliance
Lightning Source LLC
Chambersburg PA
CBHW071853160426
43209CB00003B/536